Miss Millie and the Marbles

Written by Caryn Sonberg
Illustrated by Michelle Dorenkamp

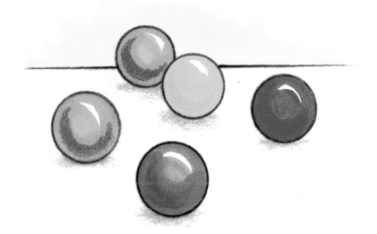

This book is dedicated to Grandma Millie, who always taught me what it meant to be a good person.
Caryn Sonberg

For my grandmothers Millie and "Pete," who taught me how to be strong and sweet, and to my granddaughter Katlyn, who reminds me to be joyful.
Michelle Dorenkamp

Ballard & Tighe

Copyright ©2005 Ballard & Tighe, Publishers, a division of Educational IDEAS, Inc. All rights reserved. No part of this publication may be reproduced in whole or in part, or stored in a retrieval system, or transmitted in any form or by any means, electronic or mechanical, including photocopy, recording, or otherwise, without permission in writing from the publisher.

2005 Printing • Cat. #2-372 • ISBN 1-55501-778-9

Editor
Dr. Roberta Stathis

Art Direction and Design
Danielle Arreola

Editorial Staff
Patrice Gotsch, Kristin Belsher, Linda Mammano, Rebecca Ratnam, Nina Chun

veryone at Stonebridge Elementary School knew Olive—the students, the teachers, and even the principal, Mr. Henry. Olive was a girl people remembered.

3

Olive was polite to adults. She always said thank you.

She was smart. She knew her ABCs.

But sometimes Olive just didn't get it.

She didn't understand the rules.

She didn't want to understand the rules.

And that's what got her into trouble.

4

It was a bright Wednesday morning.
The sun was shining through the
classroom window, making it difficult
for Olive to see the board.
"Miss Millie!" she exclaimed.
"I need to move my seat."

Before Miss Millie could say a word,
Olive had picked up her pencil, math notebook,
backpack, scissors, and a carton of crayons and
plopped herself and all her stuff down at the red
table on the other side of the classroom.

"What on earth are you doing?" shrieked Miss Millie.
"Olive, you can't just move to a new seat without permission.
You know the rules here."

But the rules didn't mean much to Olive.
"Rules, rules, rules … life would be so
much easier without rules,"
Olive muttered under
her breath.

RULES, RULES, RULES!

"Well, the sun was hurting my eyes and I can't do my work!" Olive yelled.

Miss Millie picked up Olive's belongings and sent her right back to her seat at the green table.

The other students tried not to laugh, but some just couldn't stop.
"She's bad," one little girl giggled. "She'll do anything for attention,"
another said.

Miss Millie pulled the
curtains together, making
sure the sun wouldn't disturb
Olive or any other students.
Olive just rolled her eyes
and thought out loud,
"This place would be so
much better without rules."

Clearly, Olive was in a bad mood. The sun WAS in her eyes, but she also wanted to move to the red table because they always won the most marbles. That meant they got to choose a toy out of Miss Millie's treasure chest. Olive's green table never won anything.

It just wasn't fair. Olive decided she had to find a way to win more marbles for the green table. But what could she do?

"I have to figure out how to win those marbles," Olive mumbled to herself.

After school, Olive got on the bus and sat down in an empty seat by the window. She walked right by her little brother Oliver, but she was thinking too hard to notice him. She settled into her seat and soon the wheels started turning—on the bus and in her head!

I could steal some marbles from another table.

14

Or I could pull Arthur's seat out when he tries to sit down.
That would make everyone laugh and then I could switch the
marble jars on the red and green tables. Olive smiled as she
thought of how funny it would be to pull out Arthur's seat.

When she got home, Olive went straight to her room. She was slowly beginning to formulate her master marble plan. This plan had to trick everyone. It had to confuse Miss Millie and make all the kids at her table proud. When her plan succeeded, Olive would be the hero.

Olive spent all night trying to figure out how to trick Miss Millie. She tossed and turned. She stared at the ceiling and thought her hardest. How could she outsmart Miss Millie? She knew she could. The problem was that she had to do it tomorrow. Miss Millie always counted the marbles on Friday.

Then it came to her. "My marbles," she said out loud. "I'll bring my own marbles to class. Then I'll put them into the green table's jar."

The next morning, Olive decided she'd better write down her plan. She didn't want to mix up even one step—that could ruin the whole thing.

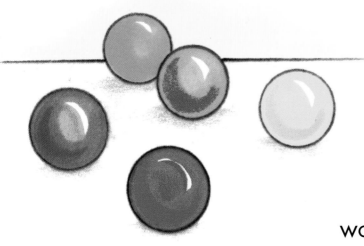

When Olive arrived at school on Thursday, she was ready to put her perfect, powerful, plain old wonderful plan into action. All day long, all she could think about was what she was going to do. She got in trouble during writing because she was staring out the window. She was sent to "time out" during math because she was drawing circles instead of subtracting two-digit numbers. She even got hit on the head with a ball during P.E. because she wasn't paying attention.

Olive's daydreaming was rudely interrupted by Mr. Henry's voice that boomed over the loud speaker: "Good afternoon, students and teachers. It is that time of the day when we prepare to go home."

The students got their coats from the closet. They filled their backpacks with papers and supplies from their cubbies. This was it … her table had to have the most marbles, and Olive knew what had to be done.

Everyone eagerly lined up. Miss Millie walked beside the line of students, making sure they were following the hallway rules.

Olive took a couple of steps into the hallway, but then quietly sneaked back into the classroom. No one was around. The classroom was very quiet—spooky quiet. Olive carefully opened her backpack, pulled out a handful of marbles, and gently placed them into the jar sitting on the green table.

21

She was done. That was it! All she had to do now was catch the bus home. As she walked out of the classroom, Olive passed Miss Millie, who smiled at her. Suddenly, Olive felt weird. She felt proud that she had pulled off her plan, but she also felt bad, like she had done something really wrong.

Olive scooted onto the bus just as the doors were closing. "There you are!" Oliver yelled from his seat.

He was sitting on his knees so he could see over the seat in front of him. "You scared me!" Oliver said as he sunk back into his seat.

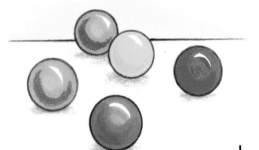

Olive didn't talk to Oliver on the bus.

When they got home, she went straight to her room and shut the door. She didn't say anything at dinner. Something inside her still didn't feel right. "I'm going to bed," Olive told her parents as she cleared the dinner plates from the kitchen table.

"Is everything all right?" her father asked. "Is there anything you want to talk about?"

"Nope. Just tired," Olive replied.

Olive tried to fall asleep, but she couldn't. She just didn't feel right. She heard the television in the living room and went to find her father. He'd know what to do. "Dad," Olive said. "I did something really bad." Olive told her father the whole story— from getting into trouble with Miss Millie, to planning a way to cheat, to passing Miss Millie in the hallway after she had gotten away with her plan. "I just don't feel right," she said, her head hanging low.

"Olive, you should feel bad," her father told her in his serious and stern voice. "What you did was dishonest and wrong. But now is your chance to learn from your mistakes."

Then Olive's father put his arm around her. In a softer voice, he said, "It is normal to want to win, but winning means putting forth your best effort. Winning means playing a fair game. First thing tomorrow, you have to tell Miss Millie what you did and then you have to apologize."

Olive's father drove her to school the next morning. Together, they walked to Olive's classroom. Olive admitted what she had done, first to Miss Millie, and then to the rest of her class. Olive's dad smiled at her.

Miss Millie listened carefully. She accepted Olive's apology and explained that cheating and lying are very bad traits. Then she talked a lot about fairness and working together toward a common goal. "To win at anything—a baseball game, a poetry contest, even a marble competition—means following the ..."

Before Miss Millie could finish her sentence,
Olive blurted out: "**THE RULES ...** you have to follow the rules."

"That's right, Olive," Miss Millie smiled.
"You have to follow the rules."

About the Author

Caryn Sonberg was born in Miami, Florida in 1977. She currently resides in Alexandria, Virginia, where she is a third-grade teacher. When she was a child, Ms. Sonberg spent many summers with her grandmother, Millie. One of her favorite memories of their time together is sitting on the couch listening to her grandmother's "Olive" stories. Each fictional story about a little girl named Olive was tied to a moral lesson. Ms. Sonberg wanted to record the Olive stories to keep her grandmother's tradition alive and share these important life lessons with children everywhere.

This is a photograph of Caryn Sonberg and her grandmother, Millie Sonberg.